P9-ARV-009

THE PEOPLE
OF NEW CHINA

THE PEOPLE
OF NEW CHINA

by MARGARET RAU

with photographs by the author

JULIAN MESSNER
New York

For Cathy

ACKNOWLEDGMENTS: I wish to credit the skillful darkroom work of veteran photojournalist Win Muldrow and his ProLab for bringing out the best in my photographs.

Design by Ruth Bornschlegel

Library of Congress Cataloging in Publication Data

Rau, Margaret.
  The people of new China

  Includes index.
    1.   China—Description and travel—1976
—Juvenile literature   1.   Title.
DS712.R38   951.05   78-960
ISBN 0-671-32870-0

CONTENTS

VILLAGE LIFE

Hsi-fan's home is in the village of Tek Ya Na, which stands on the edge of a pond in south China. There are many villages like it scattered over the countryside. The roofs of the houses are made of tile and the walls are of adobe brick, which does not last too long. None of the houses are very old, though the weathering of wind, rain and sun makes them seem that way.

Whenever a house is in need of repair, the owner buys the materials and everyone in the village helps with the work. In this way, they save a great deal of money.

Hsi-fan, her parents and older sister live in one of the houses. The rooms are built around a courtyard enclosed by a wall. These rooms are shared out among great grandfather, grandmother and grandfather, Hsi-fan and her family, an aunt and uncle and their children.

The family shares the kitchen, which has the only electric light in the house. It hangs over the kitchen table on a long cord. And to save energy, it is always turned off when not in use. The kitchen has a sink, but no running water. Hsi-fan and her cousins fill buckets with water at the village pump and carry it to the big earthenware jar which stands in one corner of the kitchen.

This typical south China village, with houses of adobe bricks roofed with tiles, stands on the edge of one of the many ponds that are scattered throughout the lower valley of the Pearl River.

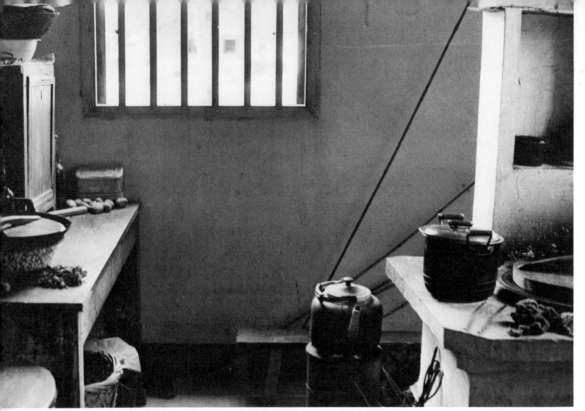

Cooking for the family is done in this kitchen on a cement stove which burns charcoal or kindling wood.

(opposite) Washing clothes on the banks of a pond is an ancient custom in the Chinese countryside, where there are no washing machines.

The village women use the pond as their laundry tub. They bring their dirty clothes to the edge of the pond, and scrub and rinse them while chatting among themselves. Once they used sand to scour the clothes, but now China makes its own soap.

After the clothes are washed, they are hung out to dry on bamboo poles, which are thrust through the sleeves of the jackets and the legs of the trousers. This smooths out the clothes so they don't have to be ironed.

Newly washed clothes are stretched out to dry on bamboo poles in front of a thatch-roofed village cottage.

(opposite) Grandparents, like this old man shelling freshwater clams for the evening meal, enjoy taking care of their grandchildren as well as making themselves useful in other ways.

Father and uncle take their turns with the cooking along with Hsi-fan's mother and aunt. But it is usually grandmother who is in charge of the meals. The cooking is done on a cement open-mouthed stove. Charcoal, dry twigs and rice stalks are used for fuel. Often Hsi-fan helps by squatting in front of the stove and fanning the fire until it burns briskly.

Cooking is done in a large iron pot, or wok, whose pointed bottom fits into a round hole cut in the top of the stove. In it grandmother fries vegetables, fish, pork and chicken while a pot of rice simmers at the back.

Though grandfather cannot cook, he helps prepare the food and minds Hsi-fan's year-old baby brother, Tai-ming. Grandfather

10

gathers freshwater mussels from the pond and nearby streams and shells them for the evening meal. Tai-ming sits beside him in his play pen—just a big wicker basket. When Tai-ming grows tired of sitting, grandfather lifts him out and plays with him for a little while before going back to work again.

The people of Tek Ya Na make their living from rice. The fields stretch far away on all sides around the village. When Hsi-fan's parents were children, the fields were broken up into small plots separated by narrow enbankments. Each plot was tilled by a family. As the years went by, the fields became smaller and smaller because the land was subdivided again and again among the male children.

Soon there was scarcely enough land in each plot to provide food for the family even in a good year. In a bad year the family ate the rice which was saved for seed. Then it had to borrow money at high interest rates to buy seed for the next planting. If another bad season came along and the family lost a second crop, it might be forced to sell one or more children to keep the heavily mortgaged land.

Girls were always the ones to be sold, because in old China, boys were considered much more important. It was they who carried on the worship of the ancestors in the ancestral hall of the clan. Today Hsi-fan's grandmother often tells her, "You are a lucky girl, Hsi-fan. You have the same rights as boys. You will never have to be sold as two of my sisters were in the old days."

"We are all lucky," great grandfather adds. "Our whole village—everyone."

Great grandfather has lived through many upheavals and seen many bad times. He managed to survive when the average age in old China was only twenty-five years. Now it is sixty-five, but great grandfather has lived far beyond this point. He is ninety-five years old, but still very spry. In his lifetime, he has seen the Manchu

This village elder is 95 years old and still very spry. He is active in village councils, where he is respected for his age and experience.

dynasty toppled from its throne, and China turn from an Empire into a Republic. He has lived through the Civil War between the Nationalists and the Communists, the Japanese invasion, and finally the victory of the Communists over the Nationalists.

Great grandfather has watched many changes taking place since the People's Republic of China was founded on October 1, 1949. He has seen the disappearance of the handkerchief-size rice plots as the peasants began to realize how much better it would be if they worked together. Pooling their land, tools, and livestock, they share the farm work and divide the profits among themselves.

Great grandfather has seen a new kind of rice taking the place of the rice of his childhood. The new rice grows a little more than half as tall as the old variety. It matures quicker so that the peasants can grow three crops a year instead of two, as in the past. It is also sturdy enough to resist diseases such as rust and mildew if the weather becomes damp.

One of the worst evils that afflict south China is the typhoon. Great grandfather has seen many of them and Hsi-fan only a few. The full fury of a typhoon seldom hits Hsi-fan's home village, but the fringe of one on its way north does occasionally sweep through the countryside causing real damage. Usually the typhoons come in the summer, but this year there was one in autumn.

Hsi-fan knows the signs that a typhoon is coming. The air is thick, hushed and oppressive. At dusk, the sky has a rosy glow— another storm sign. This glow shines over fields and village and into the mirrorlike pond.

Then all at once the wind rushes out of the sky, sometimes bringing heavy rain, sometimes just a scattering of drops. The wind whips tiles from roofs, and flattens some stands of rice, leav ing others untouched.

These school children have come to help with the rice harvesting. They will pick up stray stalks left by the reapers.

Three times a year, the harvest season comes to the village. This is the fall harvest season. Everywhere the yellow ripened fields stretch to the horizon. Many volunteers arrive from the city to help with the harvest: clerks, school teachers, students, soldiers from the nearby barracks.

Hsi-fan and her classmates are excused from school to do their share. Lined up in front of the old ancestral hall, now used as the village headquarters, the children stand patiently. Baskets over their arms, straw hats on their heads, they listen to the instructions of their teacher before marching off to the fields.

Everywhere in the countryside, there is the bustle of working people. Moving ahead of everyone are the mowers, skillfully swinging their scythes—scythes so sharp that if handled carelessly they could easily make a nasty gash, slice off a finger, or even a hand.

There are practical nurses in the fields to care for such emergencies, and to give simple remedies to those who are taken suddenly ill. The practical nurses are trustworthy villagers who have been selected by their fellow peasants. They are given a six-week training course at a hospital, and then return to their community. Though they receive no extra pay, they feel honored to have been selected for such a responsible job. The peasants refer to them proudly as their barefoot doctors because, like the other peasants, they work barefoot in the fields. But in case of need, their first-aid kits, marked by a red cross, are never far from hand.

Down the rich golden fields go the skillful mowers in a fast-moving line. Behind them come the reapers, gathering the fallen stalks of rice into sheaves or bundles and carrying them to the threshing machines. Most of the threshers are the old-fashioned kind, like the ones Chinese peasants have used for centuries. A broad circular mat is attached to a tub against which the peasant beats a sheaf of stalks, *thwack, thwack, thwack,* sending the ripe grains showering into the tub below.

However, Hsi-fan's father is operating a new kind of thresher invented by the villagers themselves. It is run by a foot pedal.

(top) This young barefoot doctor will soon be on his way to work in the fields, carrying his first-aid kit marked with a red cross.

(bottom) Wearing surgical masks to keep from breathing in dust, peasants thresh the rice with a newly invented thresher which is operated by a foot pedal.

16

When Hsi-fan's father steps on the pedal, a paddle comes up and beats against the rice stalks, knocking off the grains.

Out in the fields, elderly people mind the village buffaloes that are grazing on bits of rice stalk left behind. After the buffaloes have grazed, the now barren fields are prepared for the next planting, which will take place as soon as the rains come.

To get a good yield of rice, a great deal of fertilizer is needed. There is a shortage of the commercial kind in China so the villagers use organic materials. They have enlarged the size of their piggery not only to sell the pigs at the marketplace, but also because the manure pigs produce is both plentiful and rich.

Another source of fertilizer is the rich mud in the bed of the stream. In the dry fall season, the water in the stream has been falling lower and lower exposing the mud. Teams of young people cart this mud to the fields in wicker baskets attached to carrying poles. The mud is spread over the ground, and when the rains come the nutrients in the fertilizer will sink into the soil.

Meanwhile, as the threshing tubs fill with golden grain, it is dumped into carts and taken to the large communal courtyard in the village. The carts are made out of old lumber or bamboo poles with wheels of either rubber tires or wooden rims.

The carts are drawn by oxen or by the peasants themselves. The peasants also carry great bundles of rice stalks swinging from shoulder poles.

As the carts arrive at the village courtyard, it too becomes the scene of great activity. The threshed rice stalks are stacked into

(top) Harvested fields are having the topsoil turned in preparation for the next planting.

(bottom) Young people shovel the rich creek mud which they will spread over the fields for fertilizer.

neat piles or haystacks. Buckets full of grain are dumped into the winnowing tubs to separate the chaff. Villagers with rakes spread the grain in a thin coverlet over the courtyard floor to dry. Then it will be bagged for the market.

In the fall, the village courtyard is the scene of great activity as the harvested grain is brought in to be winnowed and dried.

Everyone has a share to do, even Hsi-fan's little cousin. She minds her baby brother while her mother and older sister work. Tied securely to her back, the baby sleeps while the little girl plays with the other children.

After the last of the rice is harvested, the accounting begins. It is done by an elected group of people—a revolutionary committee which runs the village.

The committee gives each villager a good portion of rice. Another portion is put in the village's reserve silos, or storage sheds. If a bad year should come along, the villagers can draw on these reserves. The rest of the grain will be sold to the government at prices it has fixed. A small share of the proceeds will pay the taxes. Another small share will be put aside to buy livestock and simple farm equipment, and pay for such services as retirement pensions and schools.

The rest of the money is divided among the peasants. Besides their ration of rice, each family may receive anywhere from $250 to $400 a year. But this does not make up their whole income. Each family also has a private plot where it grows vegetables. It also has several chickens or ducks and a pig. Hens, pigs, eggs and vegetables can either be eaten at home or taken to market and sold at government fixed prices. The money belongs to the family to spend or save.

The peasants work in their vegetable plots in their spare time. And Hsi-fan likes to help her mother weed and water and gather the vegetables—yard-long beans, squash, cabbages and tomatoes. She also helps take care of the chickens and the pig.

The family has already saved enough money to buy a sewing machine on which Hsi-fan's mother and grandmother sew clothes for the family. Now they are saving for a bicycle to be shared by everyone.

HSIN HUI TOWN

Tek Ya Na is only one of several villages which are united into a larger unit—the brigade. The brigade is run by a committee of men and women elected from several villages. They meet at their headquarters, which is located in a larger town. Every village gives a small amount of money to the brigade out of which old age pensions are paid to brigade members. Women get a pension when they reach the age of fifty-five, men at sixty.

The brigade also runs a clinic where barefoot doctors can bring their more seriously ill patients for diagnosis and treatment. The primary school which Hsi-fan attends is located here. Children from all the villages in the brigade think nothing of walking a mile or more to reach their school. The brigade also runs a day care center for very young children whose parents work in the field and who have no grandparents to care for them.

It is brigade money that purchases the few trucks and tractors which are shared by all the villages. The small, lightweight tractors are used for most of the plowing. Oxen-drawn plows take care of the rest.

The brigade is part of a still larger unit made up of several brigades. It is called a commune. The headquarters of the commune in which Hsi-fan lives is a town called Hsin Hui. The factory that makes the tractors is located there, and the tractors are sold at cost to the brigades.

Children are being taken care of at a village day-care center, so their parents can go to work. In earlier years, peasant mothers used to carry their children on their backs when they went into the fields.

The commune also runs a hospital where seriously ill people are taken care of. It has a House of Respect for the Aged, a kind of retirement home for those who have no relatives to care for them. And it runs a high school for the teenagers of the commune.

Hsi-fan's older sister Ming-li has just graduated from the high school in Hsin Hui. Now she is taking a six-month training course in the commune factory to repair tractors and other farm machinery. When she completes the course, she will open a small repair shop at brigade headquarters and service the farm equipment. This will save the peasants from having to bring it in to Hsin Hui, wait for it to be repaired and then take it back again—a waste of valuable time.

The people of Ming-li's brigade chose her for the important job of repair person not only because she has a mechanical turn of mind, but because she has shown herself willing to serve others. Ming-li considers their trust in her a great honor. In old China, she would never have been thought capable of such work.

Apprentices—both girls and boys—from all the other brigades in the commune are taking the course with Ming-li. She knows them well for she went to high school with them.

During the working day, the apprentices learn how to make the various parts they will need in their repairs. Older workers oversee their work, giving suggestions, correcting mistakes. At first, the apprentices were embarrassed by the many errors they made. To put them at ease, an elderly worker told them the story of the founding of the light tractor factory.

"It all began as one big mistake," he explains. "In 1952, when the peasants kept asking for tractors to help them with the plowing, some of us decided we would try to give them what they wanted. We didn't have a factory building or any machinery at the time. The central government was very poor, and we were too proud to ask it to help us, so we made a start ourselves.

"Our first factory building was just a shed. Our first machinery was castoff bits from large city factories in Kuangchow (Canton). We figured out ways to piece it together and make it work. We decided to copy a small light tractor we saw at a trade fair in Kuangchow.

24

This light tractor factory in Hsin Hui, set up in 1952, has rapidly expanded in size. The basketball court is a common sight on factory grounds around China. During their time off, workers can sink a few baskets or have a quick game.

(below) Brigade workshops such as this one, which repairs bicycles on the spot, save both time and money for the peasants.

"All the peasants in the vicinity came to look at our first tractor. We drove it down the highway and it ran very smoothly. But when we drove the tractor into a muddy field, it just stopped dead and began to sink. We had to get strong oxen to haul it out again.

"But we wouldn't give up. We wrote to other tractor factories sending them our design and asking what had gone wrong. The factories lent us seasoned workers who came and showed us how to iron out the kinks. We made a new tractor and this one worked. Now we have a regular factory building and it is expanding all the time. Just look at all the tractors we're making. We'll be able to make even more now that you're taking over the repair job for us. So don't blame yourselves for beginners' mistakes."

Because the factory apprentices put in a full day's work, they can't return to their home villages in the evening. Instead they live in a dormitory connected with the factory. During their apprenticeship, they also receive a small allowance from the government. This pays for clothing and food, both of which are inexpensive.

Throughout their work day, the young people get breaks to do various things. Their longest break comes at noon when everyone in the town, including school children, takes a siesta.

During their siesta period, Ming-li and her friends like to throw a few balls into the basketball net on the factory court. Almost every factory in China has a basketball court. And teams of factory workers play against one another and other factories.

Even the children in the nursery schools hold basketball matches on small courts with pint-size balls and low baskets. And their playgrounds are furnished with equipment like toboggan slides and pingpong tables. They play such games as tug o' war and a Chinese version of ring around the rosie.

When the basketball court is being used, Ming-li and one of her friends spend their time lobbing shuttlecocks back and forth with badminton rackets. They don't bother with a net because it's just for practice.

Three times a week, the apprentices along with the other factory workers hold political study sessions. They read the works of Communist philosophers and revolutionaries—Marx, Engels, Lenin, and their own first leader, Chairman Mao Tsetung. They discuss how best to follow Communist principles in their own lives

Games such as Tug o' War and the Chinese version of Ring Around the Rosie provide nursery children with plenty of outdoor exercise.

These young children are playing basketball on a court scaled down to their size, with a ball and baskets to match.

by serving the people better. And they criticize themselves for their shortcomings. Such discussion groups are held all over China in country villages and big cities.

Both Ming-li and her friend, Mei-hua, belong to the Communist Youth League and they have sent in their written applications for membership in the Chinese Communist Party. Not everyone is allowed to join the party. The decision is up to Party representatives who will first talk about the young women to the peasants in their home villages and to their fellow factory workers.

Becoming a Communist Party member is considered both a great honor and a very serious commitment. Members are expected to set a good example by serving wholeheartedly the people and their country.

All factory workers get one day off a week. Sometimes on her day off, Ming-li walks the ten miles to Tek Ya Na to visit with her family. She brings them small gifts, perhaps oranges or papayas or carambolas (a kind of fruit) which she buys at the local food markets.

But for grandmother's seventieth birthday, Ming-li wants something special, so she goes to the Hsin Hui palm leaf factory to purchase a fan for her. The factory looks like a two-story private house with a large courtyard. Hsin Hui is palm country. Stocky palm trees line canal and river banks and roads, and cover the slopes of some of the hills. Their thick fringed leaves gleam in the sun and rustle in every breeze.

People began planting trees here some four hundred years ago, and articles made from their leaves soon became well known around China. Once the palm leaf factory was privately owned. Now it is run by the government.

Just the thing for grandmother on a hot summer day! Ming-li buys a fan bound with tape for a few pennies.

(above) Using a special machine, workers stamp out fans from palm leaves gathered in the palm groves of Hsin Hui commune.

Elegant hats also are manufactured at the factory. They are very popular with government officials and businessmen in the tropical countries of Southeast Asia.

If she had more money, Ming-li could have bought one of the fancier palm fans with a picture of a landscape. For still more money, she could have purchased a fan with embroidered flowers or pomegranates or pandas. The most ornate and expensive fans are glazed and encased in glass for use as wall decorations. Most of the decorated fans will not be sold in China. Neither will the dressy hats of bleached palm leaves. They are for the export market, and will help bring in much-needed capital, which China can spend on new western machinery for her old factories.

Sometimes, instead of going home, Ming-li and her friends spend their free day at Jade Lake which lies almost a mile away up in the hills. Though it's a steep climb, a narrow road winding around the slope of the hills makes it easier. On their way, the young people pass groups of laughing men, women and children, all headed for an outing, too.

As far back as 147 A.D., these wooded hills have been a favorite visiting place for the people of this part of China. In the old days, an ancient Buddhist monastery and a temple were hidden among the trees. Some of the ancient records of the Sung dynasty were kept here, for the emperors often visited this spot. An old saying describing it runs, "Trees touch the sky. Mountain streams are unending."

All this changed in the 1940s when the Japanese armies invaded Hsin Hui. They destroyed the temple with all of its precious records, and cut down the trees for firewood. Soon hillslopes and valleys were turned into treeless wasteland through which the streams rushed unchecked, taking away a lot of the precious soils.

After the founding of the People's Republic of China, Chairman Mao Tsetung issued his famous statement, "Green the land." He meant "Plant trees until the land turns green." The campaign was necessary because over the centuries so many forests had been cut down all over China that there were serious soil erosion problems everywhere.

The government officials at Hsin Hui decided they would do something about their own bare slopes. First, they dammed the waters of the streams, creating a large reservoir which they called Jade Lake because of its clear green waters. They built a powerhouse which provided electricity for Hsin Hui, and dug irrigation ditches to carry the water to reclaimed farmland. They planted thousands of trees, not only pine, fir and other forest trees, but also orchards of litchi, pears, plums, and papayas.

Soon forests crowded around Jade Lake. Then the officials decided that this beautiful site should be transformed into a park for the people of Hsin Hui. They built a lunch room where visitors could buy tea and snacks for only a few pennies. They circled the lake with a footpath. Here and there along the shore, they built gay pavilions with upturned roofs, and spanned scenic spots with curved bridges.

Ming-li and her friends are proud of the green forests which clothe the hills, for they have helped plant them. It has become a community project. Year after year in the fall, the people of Hsin Hui commune gather to set out saplings, until all the barren land is covered.

Everywhere in China, countryside and city have been transformed by the greening program. Shade and fruit trees line streets and roads, rivers and canals. They shelter villages and cover hills. They march like a green wall across north China, sheltering the lush farmlands to the south from the chill Mongolian plains over which fierce gales howl. Along exposed coasts, orchards of gnarled apple trees screen newly reclaimed rice fields. And tree farms planted during the first years of the program are now beginning to provide some of the nation's lumbering needs.

Still the work continues.

KIANGMEN, BUSTLING RIVER PORT

The delta region of Kwangtung Province, in which Hsin Hui stands, is bisected by many small rivers and tributary streams. Chief among the rivers are the Si, the Pei and the Tung, which flow from the interior of China, cross Kwangtung Province and draw together in the delta region to form the Pearl River.

Barges and junks (small sail ships) still carry goods and passengers from the hinterland to the coast, stopping at river ports along the way. However, light freighters constructed on river shipyards are taking over some of the water traffic. And in the delta itself, more and more goods are being carried by truck.

The trucks cross rivers and streams on large flat-bottomed ferries. The men who run the ferries belong to a cooperative which charges each truck and passenger a small fee for its services. Out of the pooled earnings, taxes are paid and a small amount of money is set aside to take care of old-age pensions and medical expenses for the ferrymen and their families. The rest of the money is divided among the members of the cooperative.

One destination of the trucks is the lively river port of Kiangmen which stands on an arm of the Si River. Kiangmen is the processing center for the vast fields of sugarcane nearby. It also has a pulp and paperboard mill and various other small factories.

Eleven-year-old Kit-ho was born in this city of some 85,000 people. Her father is the chief-of-staff of the Kiangmen hospital and her mother is a school teacher. The family lives in an apartment on the hospital grounds. The hospital, which was built by missionaries in the early 1900s, now is run by the government. It has expanded many times since its beginning. During the years Kit-ho's father has served here, he has seen the native forms of medicine, such as acupuncture and herbal anesthesias, once regarded as superstition, now being used in his hospital and accepted around the world as valuable treatment.

Kit-ho's father is a skillful surgeon who has performed many operations using both acupuncture and herbal anesthesia. Just this morning he operated on a young woman with an enlarged goiter which was blocking her windpipe. She was given acupuncture by an anesthetist who inserted an acupuncture needle in the appropriate nerve center, effectively blocking off the pain. She remained conscious, and was able to watch her operation in a mirror placed next to her. When the operation was over, she got up and walked away. After several hours of rest, she will be back at her job.

Kit-ho's father then moved on to an older woman whose surgery was much more serious. The doctors had to remove a large tumor from her uterus. Acupuncture anesthesia would not work for her so she was given an herbal anesthesia which was administered intravenously. The doctors cut open her abdomen and removed a tumor the size of a grapefruit. The operation was successful, but the woman was not able to walk away immediately as did the young woman with the goiter operation. She must spend at least a week in the hospital before being discharged.

All kinds of operations, from brain surgery to heart surgery, are performed at the hospital. There are even operations for the restoration of severed fingers and hands and, more rarely, arms and legs. Restoring severed fingers is one of the most difficult operations, because the blood vessels which must be rejoined are so

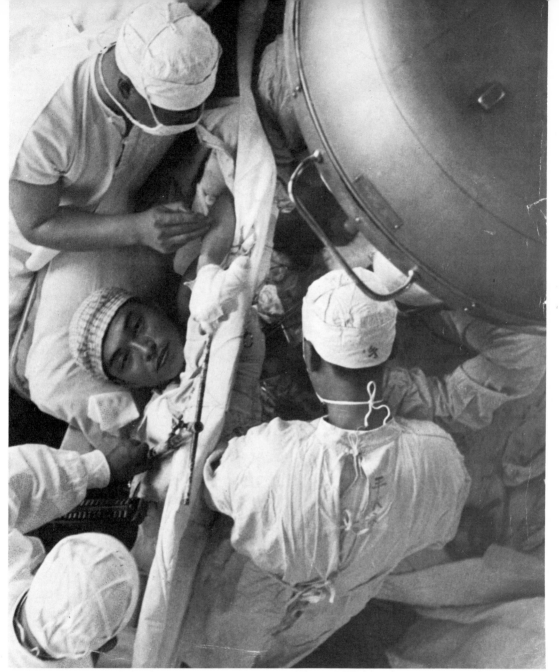

This man is having a lobe of his lung removed while under acupuncture anesthesia.

tiny. Kit-ho's father has spent many hours perfecting his skill by reuniting the tiny network of severed blood vessels in a rabbit ear.

Like all doctors in China, Kit-ho's father doesn't charge for his services but is paid a fixed salary by the government. The salaries of older doctors are among the highest in China, but they are still very low by American standards. Kit-ho's father receives about one hundred American dollars a month. But costs for food and clothing and rent are low in China too. The rent the family pays for its apartment amounts to about two and a half American dollars a month.

Except in cases of emergency, patients are not brought directly to the hospital. Most of them are referred to it by their neighborhood clinics. Like the countryside, the cities of China are divided into districts which are subdivided into neighborhoods. Each neighborhood is governed by a revolutionary committee elected from among its own members.

The committee runs a clinic where volunteers with basic training such as is given the barefoot doctors, can make health checkups, and diagnose and treat simple ailments such as colds. They also give inoculations against such diseases as smallpox, diphtheria and typhoid fever. The neighborhood clinics send patients whom they cannot handle to the hospital. The committees also conduct campaigns to remind their neighborhood people to keep their streets clean and to wage war on flies and mosquitoes.

China is very health conscious today. Nurses come to Kit-ho's school to give the children checkups. From babyhood up, they are taught the importance of cleanliness. At the day care center for preschool children, which Kit-ho's six-year-old brother, Ta-lai, attends, everyone is required to wash hands and face and brush teeth the first thing each day. Before snacks are served, the children again must wash their hands.

Through the use of puppet shows which they put on themselves, children learn the importance of cleanliness.

Ta-lai and several other older children have worked up a puppet show emphasizing the importance of cleanliness. Now and then they put it on for the other children. In the skit, a little boy named Tan never washes his hands before he eats. One day he complains of a very bad stomach ache and has to see the doctor. The doctor looks at his stomach through a fluoroscope. There is a big worm curled up inside. He tells Tan that his hands were dirty and covered with worm eggs, and that he ate them along with his food. One of the eggs has hatched into a worm. To get rid of the worm, Tan has to take some very bad-tasting medicine. He promises the doctor, his mother and all his classmates that from now on he will always wash his hands before eating.

To protect the children from malaria-carrying mosquitoes, nursery beds in these southern cities are equipped with netting which is let down and tucked around the child when it takes its afternoon nap. Today, most mosquitoes have been eliminated in China by spraying the ponds where they breed, and the malaria which they spread is now well under control. But protection against the insects is still going on.

Kiangmen is a lively city, but its pace is a leisurely one. After a morning of work, people spend their afternoon siestas in various ways. Some enjoy a leisurely game of Chinese checkers on the shady side of their office building. Others attend the local theater,

These men are enjoying the popular game of checkers during their midday siesta.

especially when a new revolutionary film comes to town. The entrance fee is only a few pennies.

When the film is over, the streets are crowded with people returning to work and children to school. Housewives stop to purchase food from the open stalls. Later, as school lets out and stores, factories and workshops close for the day, the crowds again fill the streets. By dusk, the streets are almost empty. Most of the people are at home eating.

As the night deepens, the crowing of the roosters begins. In most countries, roosters crow at dawn, but in Kiangmen they start at twilight and continue on throughout the night. The crowing can be heard everywhere because people like to keep their fowl on the slightly sloping roofs of their homes, many of which are two stories high. Here the roosters crow and the hens cluck and lay their eggs. And they all strut around pecking at the food scraps and grain tossed out on the roof.

On warm summer evenings, people like to sit on the upper balconies of their homes. Fanning themselves to keep cool, they chatter and laugh through the early night hours. Someone brings out a *pi pa*, which is a Chinese fiddlelike instrument, and begins to play. Someone else starts singing. Often it's eleven o'clock before the laughter, the singing and the pi pa playing die away as the people of Kiangmen go to sleep for the night.

With the first light of dawn, the city begins to bustle again. On a rooftop, a man starts exercising. Another squats by a bucket of water brushing his teeth. Afterwards he washes face, neck and arms and is ready for the day. A young woman sits at an upper window combing and braiding her long black hair. Children squeal and laugh and upset their mothers by wriggling as they get dressed.

Down on the streets, people on bicycles, bells clanging, pedal briskly to work. Kit-ho and her classmates join the crowds as they hurry down the curved streets, which follow the shape of the river on which the city stands. They are on their way to school which starts promptly at eight-thirty.

Kit-ho's path runs beside the river. Sometimes after school, she likes to stop here and watch the river life moving past. Now a stately junk glides by, brown sails spread. A white river freighter

The curved streets of Kiangmen parallel the contours of the river on which the city stands.

cuts the water, leaving behind a streamlined wake. Occasionally a houseboat draws up to the wharf unloading bags of herbs or bundles of sugarcane gathered in the back country for the hospital or the factory.

The barge is the home of river people. The family sleeps in the bunks in the hold. The hold (space in the bottom of the boat) is covered over with boards during the day time. The cooking is done in a little charcoal brazier in the stern of the boat. Morning and evening, the fragrant odor of cooking rice, some vegetables and fish mingled with the pungent smell of charcoal smoke floats over the river.

Sitting cross-legged on the deck, the family eats their meals with chopsticks. They will stay several days reloading the barge before continuing downstream to stop at other towns along the way.

Every time a barge ties up here, a school teacher comes to the dock to tutor the children aboard it. They learn how to read and write and do simple arithmetic sums. When the barge continues downstream, another teacher will be waiting at the next stop. In its efforts to bring education to every child in China, the government provides these tutors. Sometimes a tutor will even travel with the family.

River boat families were never so well treated in the past. Once fleets of squalid houseboats, including three-foot-wide sampans, clustered along the shores of the rivers. Whole families had to live crowded together on these tiny boats. And small children were roped to the masts or sides to keep them from falling overboard.

In the old days, the river families eked out a living ferrying passengers and goods from port to port and shore to shore. They also begged, or lived on river garbage, with now and then a fish they were able to catch. People who lived on land despised them

A few families still live on houseboats which carry produce, goods and passengers to the river towns of south China.

and would not allow them to go ashore.

The boat people lived and died aboard their crowded boats. They weren't even permitted to bury their dead on land. But since they could not bear to show their loved ones such disrespect, they would wait until midnight and then carry the corpse to a secret grave in the hills.

All this was changed after the People's Republic of China came to power. Apartment buildings were built for the boat people who were then brought ashore and given good jobs. Their children were sent to school along with the children of the land people.

Today, most of the houseboats have disappeared from the rivers. And few people think about the fact that their friendly neighbors are the formerly despised river folk.

KUANGCHOW, LARGEST CITY IN THE SOUTH

Chu-lai lives in the port city of Kuangchow, or Canton as it is known to the western world. Kuangchow, located near the mouth of the Pearl River, is the largest city in south China, containing some two million people.

Aside from several wide tree-lined boulevards, its streets are narrow and bordered with arcades where vegetables, basketware and crockery are displayed. The shops all have open fronts. Here a proprietor stands before shelves of tinned goods, behind a counter containing glass jars full of cookies. A group of school children make careful selections from the heap of sugarcane stalks that lie on the pavement in front of the shop, priced at only a few pennies each. The children strip away the outer husk with their teeth and chew on the soft sweet fiber inside.

The shop is owned and run by the man and his family. Though most businesses in China today are either operated by the government or by cooperatives, some private ownership continues. But the owner is not allowed to hire employees. He and his family must do the work themselves.

In another open shop, a woman is grinding and packaging meat for sale. And in the third, women seated in front of sewing machines are making children's clothes. The women live in the neighborhood and have formed their own cooperative. The state

44

Customers stream through the arcades of a Kuangchow shopping district, stopping to buy vegetables, meat, basketware or cooking utensils.

The proprietor of this small shop owns and runs it with the help of his family. He is not allowed to hire employees.

will buy the clothes for sale in the large government-run department stores. After they have subtracted expenses, the women will divide the rest of their earnings among themselves.

Through the arcades and down the center of the street comes a never-ending procession of people in jackets and trousers. Broad-brimmed straw hats are a common sight, for Kuangchow is hot and humid, especially in the summertime.

46

Many of the people are riding bicycles and there are a few pedicabs which have taken the place of the old two-wheel rickshaws. Men used to harness themselves in the shafts of the two-wheeled carriages and pull them. Now three-wheel pedicabs are drawn by men who sit up front and steer. They are used mainly by the elderly or the sick, or by people with small children or carrying heavy packages.

Chu-lai's home stands on one of the narrow lanes of Kuangchow. The old house, which has been repaired many times, has been passed down through the family for generations. It is occupied now by Chu-lai's grandfather, grandmother, two aunts, one uncle and their children, as well as Chu-lai's family.

In all the major cities of China, three-wheel pedicabs like these have replaced the old two-wheel rickshaws. Instead of harnessing themselves in the shafts and running on foot, pedicab drivers sit up front and pedal their fares.

The government allows a family to live in a house without paying rent or taxes, if it is fully occupied. Otherwise they must pay rent. There are so many people in China that housing is a problem and all available space is used.

As in the country homes, there is just a single electric light bulb, which hangs in the kitchen. Cooking is done on a cement range, and the house has no plumbing.

The toilet is a large earthenware crock. Every morning, very early, the crock is set outside the gate of the house joining a row of other crocks along the street. At dawn, "night-soil" men rattle by with their three-wheeled trucks collecting the contents of the crocks. They haul their loads to the country where they are dumped into compost pits to be used for fertilizer.

Water comes from a faucet in the lane nearby. For hot baths, which are taken in large wooden tubs, water is heated on the kitchen range. The laundry is also done in a wooden tub.

Almost everyone in Chu-lai's family works. His father is a foreman in the heavy machinery factory where mining and metallurgical machinery and sugar refining equipment are manufactured. Before the founding of the People's Republic, the heavy machinery factory was a very small mill with fewer than one hundred workmen and it made only simple agricultural tools. Today it is already a major industrial plant and is still expanding.

Chu-lai's uncle works with his father. His mother is one of a team of city people who are paid by the government to keep the streets clean. Early every morning, she and her team of three set out with their wheelbarrows and brooms to sweep up any trash that may have accumulated in the streets where they work. Other teams take care of other districts so that the whole city is covered.

It is hot, dusty work, and around nine o'clock Chu-lai's mother and her team take a break in the shade of some trees.

The work of the street cleaners is considered very important in

Women street cleaners take a break from their hot dusty work to refresh themselves with sips of hot water from their thermos bottles, and to do a little knitting.

China because of the emphasis on cleanliness being placed by the government. Trash cans stand along the streets, and people are encouraged to throw their litter into them.

Once the city was one of the dirtiest in China. Piles of rubbish were stacked in the streets. People threw slop from upstairs windows, and only the arcades protected the passersby. The odor of garbage hung on the air. There were frequent epidemics of cholera and bubonic plague.

Now thanks to the work of the street cleaners and the educational program carried on in every neighborhood, the streets and lanes of Kuangchow are spotless. And there is no let-up in the campaign.

Chu-lai's grandmother plays an active part in it. She is retired now and living on a pension so she can give full time to volunteer work with the neighborhood committee. She leads campaigns against flies. Arming every child with a swatter, she holds contests to see who can get the most flies. Similar contests are held all over the city, reducing the number of flies by the thousands.

Grandmother has other duties. Because there are more than 800 million people in China today, the government is concerned that unless something is done to curb the population growth, there will not be enough food for everyone. So it has launched a gigantic birth control campaign.

Grandmother is working on this campaign. She passes out information on how women can practice birth control. She urges young people to wait until they are in their late twenties before they marry and begin their families. She impresses on those already married the need to limit their children to two in a family. It is much easier to get young city couples to practice birth control than the peasants to whom traditionally sons have always been most important.

Another of grandmother's duties is to act as mediator in neighborhood and family disputes, and to organize other elderly people to help tutor the children who are falling behind in their school work. Grandmother also attends the political study meetings which are held several nights a week in the community hall.

Chu-lai's youngest aunt, Lai Feng, attends the Teachers' Institute which is just outside the city. Some 3,800 students go to the Institute. When they graduate after two years, they will be qualified teachers. But they will still not be enough for China's educational needs. And most of the teachers, especially those who teach the elementary grades, will continue to be only high school graduates.

However, Chu-lai's teacher was trained at the Institute, and she gives her students lessons in English, which has now become just about the most important foreign language in China. Already, Chu-lai can speak a few English sentences.

For centuries, Kuangchow has been one of China's main gateways to the western world. In earlier years, Hindu, Persian and Arab traders came with their wares. They were followed by Portuguese, French, Spanish, British, Dutch and Americans. The French were especially powerful in Kuangchow. They obtained a concession on an island in the Pearl River, and did not allow any Chinese to enter. The colonial-style buildings still stand, but today only Chinese use them.

When China was weak, foreign businessmen were able to force their goods—at one time principally opium products—on the Chinese. Today, China is strong and though businessmen are still welcome in Kuangchow, they are not permitted to come and go as they please. They arrive by invitation only from the Chinese government which selects those it feels are interested in making large purchases of its goods.

Foreign businessmen enter China through the British port of Hong Kong. They are greeted by guides who accompany them on the train trip to Kuangchow. Here they stay in a huge hotel built for foreign visitors. The hotel, which stands on a broad avenue, is equipped with all the modern conveniences that westerners are used to, including running water, plumbing and electricity, elevators and restaurants. Every room has a western-style toilet and bathtub.

Outside the hotel, a row of taxicabs is drawn up for the use of the foreigners. But they will spend most of their time at the great Trade Fair building across the street from the hotel. Here products brought from all over China are displayed.

On the grounds outside, there are rows of Chinese-made tractors, along with trucks and cars, and farm and factory machinery. These products, which are sold much more cheaply than those of other countries, especially attract visitors from the underdeveloped countries of Africa and southeast Asia.

In the spacious halls inside, there are displays of textiles, mats, baskets, woven rugs, porcelain, embroideries, toys, carvings of jade, ivory and stone, and lacquerwork. One lacquerwork screen shows a handsome peacock with a spread tail ornamented with iridescent mother-of-pearl disks. It took the young apprentice several months to create it.

After the visitors have looked at the various products and decided which ones they can sell in their own countries, they meet with Chinese representatives to negotiate deals. Negotiations are carried on in a leisurely fashion at little tables tucked away in alcoves, and tea is served by smiling young women in black braids. Finally contracts are signed. Sometimes, however, if the deal is a big one, businessmen are invited north to Shanghai or the capital at Peking for further discussion.

Chu-lai's teacher sometimes takes her class to the great trade hall to see the wealth of articles their country has produced. Chu-lai has been coming here ever since he entered the first

It took a young apprentice several months to complete this beautiful lacquer screen now being exhibited at the Trade Fair building in Kuangchow. Six layers of lacquer and glittering mother-of-pearl inlays have been used to create this peacock with spread tail.

grade at the age of seven. In the four years since then, he has seen the number of products steadily growing.

At every visit, his class has always stopped before the lighted model of a commune, which is called Tachai, located in a very poor section of northwest China. It is famous throughout the country because one year when a number of floods struck the little community, the peasants refused to accept government help to rebuild their ruined fields. Instead, they took great pride in living off their small amount of reserve money while doing all the work themselves. Since then, they have planted trees, terraced more hills, even built an aqueduct to be sure they would have water in their often drought-stricken area. Today they are a prosperous community.

Because China still is very poor, other communes are being urged to follow Tachai's example. And the slogan, "Learn from Tachai," is heard everywhere in the countryside.

Another model which the children always visit is one of the Taching oil fields which are located in the Northeast Region. Like the peasants of Tachai, the oil field workers and their families provided for themselves in every way. They built their own homes, shops and school centers. Rather than ask for provisions from the government, the wives and children of the drillers tilled the surrounding land and planted wheat and vegetables, and raised livestock. Now the Taching oil fields are able to care for themselves.

The people of Kuangchow are proud of their city's revolutionary history. It was in this area that the famous leader, Hung Hsiu-chüan, started a popular rebellion in 1850. It was called the great Taiping Rebellion, and it would have overthrown the corrupt Ching dynasty if the foreigners had not come to the aid of the emperor.

It was from Kuangchow, too, that Dr. Sun Yat-sen launched his Dare-to-Die revolutionary movement which did overthrow the Ching dynasty. But when Sun Yat-sen's new government was threatened by the powerful Ching general, Yüan Shih-kai, whom it had mistakenly chosen to be president, Dr. Sun and his Nationalists had to retreat to Kuangchow. It was here in 1923 that the Nationalists and the newly formed Chinese Communist Party joined forces to drive out the warlords who, after Yüan's death, had taken over China and were fighting among themselves.

Chu-lai and his class sometimes visit the historic Peasants' Institute, which was founded in Kuangchow to teach peasant recruits guerrilla warfare. One of their instructors was then a young man named Mao Tsetung, later to become the powerful chairman of the People's Republic of China. A portrait of young Mao hangs on the wall of one of the rooms.

As the guide takes the class through the Institute, she points out the various other objects of interest. Here is the room where Mao Tsetung slept. There are the barracks of the peasant trainees. The large room is equipped with individual cots and wash basins. This is the classroom where they were instructed. The guide points to the portraits of two young Chinese hanging on the wall.

"These were martyrs to the cause," she tells them. "There were many like them who lost their lives to bring the People's Republic into being. We must follow in their footsteps and serve our country as loyally."

Chu-lai and his family often visit another historic spot in their country's revolutionary history. It is called the Park of the Martyrs, and contains the mass grave of some five thousand men, women and children who were massacred by the Nationalists because they were suspected of sympathizing with the Communist cause. This happened after the Nationalists and the Communists split apart and engaged in a fierce civil war.

Once the mass grave lay in wastelands. Now it is the central point of a beautiful park. The grassy mound is surrounded by a granite railing guarded by stone lions. Around the mound stretch rolling meadows dotted with pavilions. Quiet birch woods cast their speckled shade over the meandering paths which are kept spotlessly clean by the park attendants. Trees and shrubs are pruned, fallen leaves and twigs are raked up and placed into wheelbarrows and hauled away. The debris will be used to heat kitchen stoves. In the city as in the country nothing is ever wasted.

Beyond the birch woods lies a small artificial lake where for a

In the birch woods of Martyrs' Park, attendants rake up leaves and twigs, which will be used as fuel in cooking stoves.

few pennies Chu-lai's father can rent a boat and take the family rowing. Grandmother, who doesn't care about boating, likes to sit on a bench by the water's edge just watching her family and thinking about the past.

When the boating is over, the family stops for a cold drink at one of the little snack pavilions on the lake shore. Then they are ready for home. Leaving the park, they pass the great mound and the plaque which bears Mao Tsetung's tribute to the fallen: "Marching through the blood of our comrades, we press on to victory."

Grandmother always stops to read the words slowly aloud. And her eyes mist over with a long ago memory, for in that quiet mound lie the bones of her father, her mother and two brothers.

SHANGHAI, QUEEN OF ASIA

Halfway up the China coast from Kuangchow, on the delta of the great Yangtze River, or Long River as the Chinese call it, stands Shanghai, the largest city of China, and indeed of all Asia. Hai-feng, who has lived here all her twelve years, is proud of her city, which is unique in China. Unlike other Chinese cities, it has a strong western flavor, with its victorian-style buildings and twenty-two-story skyscrapers.

Shanghai is over 800 years old, but until the British came in 1843, it was just a small village. After the British victory in the First Opium War, they expanded the town, building on land given to them along the Whangpoo River, a short tributary of the Yangtze. Shanghai was administered by foreign laws. It was almost a western island in the rich heartland of China.

Shanghai grew quickly. Soon ships of many nations were bringing goods from around the world, and taking away Chinese products, mainly tea and silk. The docks and narrow gangplanks swarmed with men loading and unloading cargo.

Chinese workers put in long, hard days for low wages. Because there was so much cheap labor available, the foreigners took advantage of the silk worm breeding which was being carried on in the surrounding countryside, and built textile mills. Native businessmen quickly established mills of their own.

Workers were paid only a few pennies a day in wages. Women and children received even less. If workers became ill or women

Unlike other Chinese cities, Shanghai was built by foreign architects and has a distinctly western flavor. But the traffic cop in the kiosk (on the left), directing the swarms of bicycles, is a typical scene of new China.

became pregnant, they were immediately fired. There were always plenty of others to take their place, for starving peasants were flocking to the city, hoping to get a job. In the Chinese sections, shacks sprang up on the dirt ground. The only shelter many families had was a piece of bamboo matting which they stretched over themselves at nightfall.

Thousands lived on swarms of old, leaky houseboats moored in Soochow Creek which flows into the Whangpoo. The water supply of the native quarter came from the filthy creek. There were

On the Whangpoo River on which Shanghai stands, modern steamers share the waterway with junks that have been sailing here for centuries.

frequent epidemics with as many as two hundred or more corpses picked up by the police each day.

Yet, with all this poverty, Shanghai was also a wealthy city. Much of its money came from drugs. Rows of opium dens sprang up along the narrow winding streets.

Shanghai bred a special kind of worker—tough and cocky. These workers had become so skilled that the businessmen couldn't do without them. When manufacturers began branching out into other fields, they found it was cheaper to send the raw goods to Shanghai where the workers were, rather than move to where materials were more easily available.

In 1921, a few Communists, including Mao Tsetung, met secretly in Shanghai to set up the Chinese Communist Party. Realizing the power the Shanghai workers held, Party organizers rallied

60

them to stage mass strikes that stopped all work in the whole city. Some of these strikes occurred when the Nationalist leader, Chiang Kai-shek, assisted by the Communists, marched north against the war lords. Chiang, who was secretly with the businessmen and landlords, celebrated his entry into Shanghai by ordering the massacre of thousands of Communists and workers. Then the Communists and Nationalists split and began to fight each other.

After the Communists established the People's Republic of China, a massive cleanup job was begun in the city. Foreign businesses were taken over by the government. Native ones were put under strict supervision. Working conditions and wages were improved. Opium dens were abolished. Opium addicts were helped to overcome their habit, and were given medical care. Old, crowded houseboats were cleared from Soochow Creek, and the worst slums were torn down, giving way to neat rows of apartment buildings.

The city has been continually expanding since then. Today a giant Shanghai shipyard is turning out cargo vessels and ocean liners. In the suburbs around the city, new factories have sprung up. The factories are surrounded by groups of apartment buildings with shopping centers, day nurseries, schools and community halls. Altogether, some ten million people live in Shanghai, which includes the surrounding suburbs and communes.

Hai-feng's home is in the inner city. Though there are still many old houses in Shanghai, Hai-feng and her family live in a more modern apartment building. It has two rooms. The living room is shared by Hai-feng and her older sister, Kuang-tien. The bedroom is used by their parents. The family shares the bathroom and kitchen with another family.

The apartment building is equipped with electricity, running water, and natural gas which is used for cooking. The rent is about $1.50 a month, with another dollar a month for gas. The water costs around twenty-five cents and electricity about fifty cents a month. Clothes are washed by hand and hung to dry on bamboo poles sticking out of apartment building windows.

Both Hai-feng's parents work in city factories. Today women are being encouraged to take factory jobs. This not only increases China's work force and the incomes of families, but it also wins women greater respect from their husbands. They have come to recognize the value of their wives as wage earners and to accept them more readily as equals.

Between them, Hai-feng's parents earn about one hundred dollars a month. Out of this, they are able to lay a little away. They

There is a homey atmosphere about this small apartment living room with its table, chairs, sideboard and sewing machine. The bed in the corner serves as a sofa in the daytime. Curtains, pictures and flowers reveal the simple but not spartan life of the occupants.

These apartment complexes for Shanghai workers have been built since the founding of the People's Republic of China. Bamboo poles sticking out from apartment windows serve as clotheslines.

have also bought a bicycle and a sewing machine, and are saving up to purchase their own furniture. Meanwhile, they rent furniture cheaply from the government. Their table costs them about a half-cent a month, the four chairs another half-cent, and the beds a half-cent each.

Medical care is no problem for the family. Both Hai-feng's parents are insured at the factories where they are employed. For a few cents a year, the workers receive free medical and dental care while their families are treated at half cost. But all fees are low. The most expensive operation costs about fifteen dollars American money.

The women of new China receive special consideration. In their

last months of pregnancy, they are not permitted to do hard
manual work, and they do not lose their wages. After the birth of
the child, they are given fifty-seven days off with full pay. When
they return to work, they can place their children in the nursery
which is run by almost every factory. Hai-feng spent the first six
years of her life in a factory nursery.

**Women are encouraged to take factory jobs, not only to increase China's work
force, but also to win greater respect from their husbands who come to recognize
their value as wage earners.**

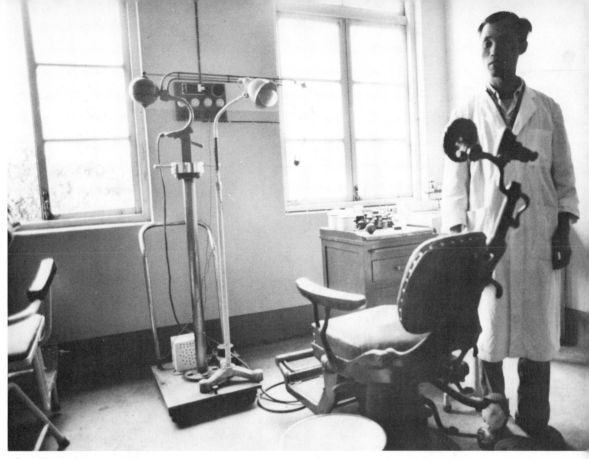

Though clinics in poor brigades may be equipped with old-fashioned machinery, the dentists who run them do careful work.

Her older sister, Kuang-tien, is studying to be a dentist at the large hospital dental school, where fifty percent of her classmates are women. In the old days, only the rich could afford to go to dentists. For everyone else, it was the local toothpuller whose only tool was a hammer to knock out the tooth. His patient sat upon a stool which he set up in the street.

Today, dental clinics have been established in cities and in many commune headquarters. Clinics in out-of-the-way places may be equipped with old-fashioned instruments, but the dentists who use them do careful work.

In a factory nursery, afternoon naps are taken in pint-size beds equipped with nettings, which are let down and tucked around the children to keep out mosquitoes.

Kuang-tien learns how to examine teeth, take x-rays and fill cavities. She also practices making sets of false teeth for those who have lost their own. The sets cost workers nothing at all. Others are charged only ten dollars for the set and the fitting.

Every six months, Kuang-tien and her team of fellow students visit schools and factories in the district, giving routine checkups and doing minor dental work. They also educate the children on dental care and provide them with toothpaste. Those who need more work on their teeth must go to the hospital. Instead of using Novocain to deaden the tooth nerve, the dentists use acupuncture. Kuang-tien knows how to place the needles at the right spot in her patients' hands.

Now in her second year as a dental school student, Kuang-tien is beginning to go down to the countryside for two months at a time to examine the peasants' teeth and do fillings. One of her chores is to teach the barefoot doctors how to handle minor dental problems.

Hai-feng and her family are all early risers. Everyone in Shanghai seems to be up before dawn. In the stillness of the night, voices can be heard in the street below, along with the ringing of bells and the clatter of carts. Peasants from the outlying communes are bringing in their produce to the city markets.

By six-thirty, Hai-feng has left her apartment to join a group of school friends who are gathering for some calisthenics. Nowhere in China is physical education taken more seriously than in Shanghai. The bund, or promenade, along the Whangpoo River is a favorite exercise ground. Older people are doing the fluid movements of Tai chi chuan, which is supposed to harmonize the

Led by a gentleman wielding a tasseled baton, these elderly people are doing the *Tai chi chuan* as their early morning exercise.

Early morning risers shop for fish and vegetables at open stalls in the narrow side streets of Shanghai.

body. An elderly gentleman using a tasseled baton directs them.

The calisthenics of the younger people are more strenuous. After warming up with a few kicks and stretching movements, Hai-feng and her friends join other children who are practicing cartwheels.

By the time Hai-feng is ready for school, her parents have already gone to work. Dressed in simple jacket and trousers and soft sneakers, Hai-feng sets out with her school bag over her shoulder. By this time, the whole city has awakened. In the narrow side streets where freshly caught shrimp and fish and newly picked vegetables have been spread out on trays, shoppers, baskets over their arms, pick and choose.

On the wide main streets, where there are no private cars, buses crammed with commuters rumble along. And riders on bicycles swoop by with a clanging of bells. Pedestrians must step lively to keep out of their way.

In a kiosk above the traffic, an officer with a megaphone directs traffic. Sometimes there's an accident. The policeman comes to investigate. Quickly a crowd gathers. Both parties to the accident tell their story and blame is fixed. If there are any damages, the guilty party must pay for repairs, which are not expensive in China. If, however, the responsible person is also guilty of breaking the law, he may have to stand trial. Trials are conducted in open court with the audience acting as jury.

Hai-feng has to board a bus to ride to her school. She joins a line of children who are buying their tickets. There are some 1,400

School children wait for a bus to take them to their school in Shanghai.

students in Hai-feng's school, which is staffed with sixty teachers.

Classes begin at eight in the morning. The curriculum consists of Chinese language lessons, mathematics, singing, art, foreign languages, history and political science. The classes are forty minutes long with a ten-minute break between each. Calisthenics on the school grounds begin the day. Physical education and sports are also stressed at recess periods and during the supervised playtime after school. During this time, from three to five in the afternoon, courses in ballet and gymnastics as well as ancient Chinese martial arts such as kung fu and wushu are given by qualified teachers.

Occasionally, Hai-feng's 6th grade class, along with the 5th grade, visits factories or communes where the students do manual work. The lower grades also do some manual work, but in their

(opposite page) Young children in day-care centers learn how to plant and tend their nursery garden.

(right) This after-school class in gymnastics is being coached by a qualified teacher.

(below) Girls doing *wushu*, the Chinese version of fencing.

classrooms. Generally it consists of assembling boxes or parts for radios. Even pre-schoolers at day-care centers have their chores. Often they weed and water a little garden which they have planted themselves. When the vegetables are ready for picking, the children gather them and the nursery cooks prepare and serve them at lunch time. Through such practical demonstrations, the children are expected to learn respect both for work and for those who perform it.

Hai-feng's school lets out at noon when the children are given a siesta that lasts till 1:30. Hai-feng's parents do not always return for lunch, but she can manage by herself. For a few pennies, she buys a filling meal at the neighborhood canteen. Frequently she spends her free time shopping for food for the family's evening dinner.

Whoever gets home first prepares the food. Sometimes Hai-feng or her mother helps her sister cook. And sometimes even her father takes his turn in the kitchen. Chinese fathers are doing their share of more and more household duties, often spending their day off caring for the children.

During six weeks in the spring, Hai-feng is seldom home early enough to help with the meal. Throughout that time, she attends the Children's Palace after school. Every city district has its own Children's Palace, and certain children are sent there from different schools in the district.

The children play games and take part in obstacle races. But a good deal of the time is spent on hobbies. The children do what interests them. Some build model ships or airplanes. Others form a team which writes and performs dramatic skits. Still others take singing and dancing lessons from qualified teachers. Two orchestras are practicing in different rooms. The children are expected to take the new skills they learn at the Palace back to their schools. During after-school activities, which last from three to five in the

On their day off from work, Chinese fathers spend time with their children, taking them on bicycle rides around the city.

afternoon, they will teach them to any classmates who are interested.

Hai-feng has joined an orchestra made up of children playing either the *pi pa* or the butterfly harp, the Chinese version of a dulcimer. Instruments are lent free by the school. Hai-feng has been playing the *pi pa* for two years and is quite skilled at it.

73

Eight-year-old Chin-mai, who plays the piano, practices on her own at home. Her parents have given up many things to save up enough money to buy the piano, though it cost them seven hundred American dollars. A piano is one of the very few expensive items in China today.

Chin-mai already can play Bach and Chopin classics as well as Chinese compositions such as "The Yellow River" concerto. She has a great deal of talent, and when she is ten years old will probably be admitted to the Conservatory of Music to complete her musical education. On graduating from the conservatory, she will become a member of one of the professional orchestras which are paid by the government to tour the country.

Other children who have good voices or special ballet talents also will receive their education in specialized schools. When they graduate, they too will become professional performers for the government.

It is late afternoon when Hai-feng leaves the Children's Palace to return home. Once again, Shanghai is crowded with workers, this time homeward bound. If the air is hot and still, a heavy blue haze hangs over the city roofs causing Hai-feng's eyes and throat to smart. Like every other heavily industrialized city, Shanghai has a pollution problem.

Hai-feng's cousin, along with other scientists, has made some headway to solve the problem. Waste water is now treated and then used for irrigation purposes. Poisonous gases are trapped and recycled instead of being released into the air as before. But the work is far from completed yet.

Evenings are often times of excursion for Hai-feng and her family. There is always something to do. They can watch television on the public television set in their neighborhood hall or go to a movie house to see a revolutionary film. Or they can attend a live concert, ballet, Chinese opera or sports event which may be appearing somewhere in the city. And there is always the Adult Cultural Palace where for a few pennies the whole family can play basketball or table tennis, or watch amateur shows.

Hai-feng may not always have this wealth of entertainment to choose from. Shanghai workers, noted for their skill, are in demand all over China. And there has been talk that Hai-feng's parents along with several other veteran workers may be transferred to a new industrial complex being established in the bleak, sparsely settled countryside of northwest China. Hai-feng's parents explain to her that it is a sacrifice they must all be willing to make to help their nation further its industrialization program.

(opposite) Students playing native instruments such as the pi pa and the butterfly harp, a type of dulcimer, have formed a children's orchestra which puts on amateur concerts.

WUSIH ON THE GRAND CANAL

Tsung-meng lives in the industrial city of Wusih which is 50 miles west of Shanghai. It stands on the shores of Lake Taihu and is bisected by the Grand Canal. The delta region in which Wusih lies is known as the Land of Fish and Rice because rice is the chief crop and fish abound in the lakes, streams and canals which interlace the land.

The Grand Canal is the chief north-south waterway of the area. In the south it ends at Hangchow which was once the summer capital of the emperors. From Hangchow, the canal snakes north through Soochow, once a favorite stopping-off place for the emperors on their journeys from their northern capitals. From Soochow, it continues on through Wusih, crosses the Yangtze, then the Huai and finally the Yellow River to reach the Chinese capital Peking.

During the later years of the empire, the canal was not used. But after the People's Republic of China was founded, it was dredged and repaired. Today it is again heavily traveled by barges carrying goods to the cities and towns along its banks.

Wusih is one of the most important of the canal cities. Located in the basin of Lake Taihu, it has become a major textile and food processing center for the summer rice and winter wheat grown here and for the products of sericulture, or the breeding of silkworms. And because of the large thermal power station which was built nearby, it is also becoming industrialized. Factories

Old gray houses line the banks of the Grand Canal, in Wusih. The canal was built in the time of the Sui dynasty emperors (589 – 618 A.D.), and still serves as China's principal north-south inland waterway.

manufacturing such heavy industry equipment as machine tools and diesel engines have been springing up in its suburbs.

Tsung-meng lives in the heart of Wusih. His home is one of a row of old gray houses that stand on the bank of the Grand Canal. A flight of stone steps leading down to the water enables his mother and older sisters to do the family laundry. They can also shop for vegetables and fish from barges which carry the products of cooperative food stores right to their door.

Tsung-meng's mother and sisters work in one of the city's silk

77

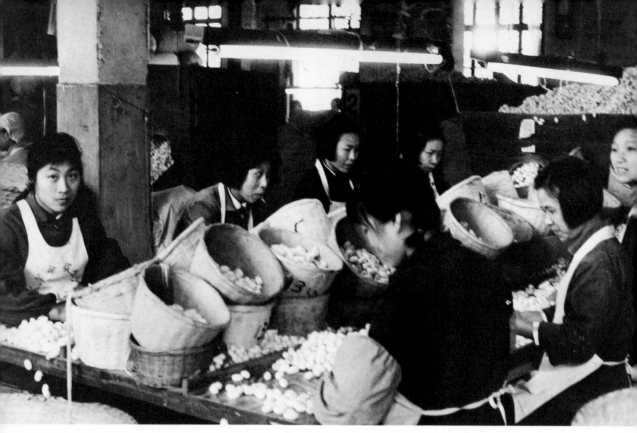

(above) Wusih is a center for the silk processing industry. Silkworm cocoons are brought to the city from the surrounding countryside. In this plant, the cocoons are sorted, and all the bad ones are thrown away.

Workers at right dip cocoons in boiling water to kill the worms and loosen the strands of silk which the cocoons are made of. The silk strands are unwound, and several are then twisted together on machines to form silk thread. The thread is shipped mostly to Shanghai textile mills where it is used to make cloth.

processing plants which prepare thousands of silkworm cocoons for the Shanghai textile mills. His father is employed in the diesel engine factory. But he is not working now. He had an accident at the plant which required an operation. After surgery, the doctor recommended that he go to the Wusih Workers' Sanitarium for more therapy.

The sanitarium is for the exclusive use of workers recuperating from operations or suffering from such chronic ailments as heart and vascular diseases, arthritis and asthma. Patients with infectious diseases are not admitted.

Because the sanitarium has only a certain number of beds, it will accept only those who have recommendations both from the doctors and their fellow workers. Then if there is an available bed, they will be admitted. Fortunately, Tsung-meng's father is one of the lucky few.

The workers' sanitarium stands in beautiful wooded country. The buildings are airy and neat and are operated by a staff of one hundred and thirty. Fifty of these are medical personnel.

The length of stay here lasts from three to six months during which the patients are checked daily by staff doctors who recommend their therapy. It ranges from western-type physical therapy to various forms of Chinese treatment, such as the use of suction cups to stimulate circulation, and acupuncture for various conditions such as arthritis.

During their stay, the patients, who continue to receive their full wages, know they will get their jobs back when they leave. To make life pleasanter and more meaningful for them while they are convalescing, they are encouraged to take part in various recreational activities which the sanitarium provides.

Tsung-meng always accompanies his mother when she visits his father. Tsung-meng's older brother, Lai-wen, does not come so often. He has just graduated from high school and is now working at a nearby commune.

The commune, which borders on Lake Taihu, has seven production brigades, and Lai-wen is stationed in the one known as the Ho La Production Brigade. It has almost two thousand members who are divided up into eighteen production teams. Eight of the teams take care of planting and harvesting the two rice crops

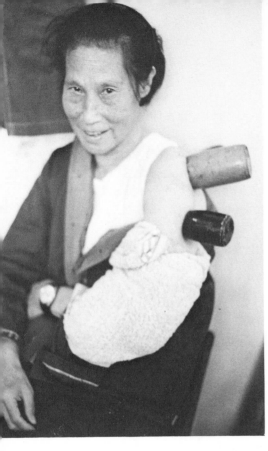

The use of suction cups to stimulate circulation is an ancient Chinese practice which is included as part of the therapy at this Wusih Workers' Sanitarium.

and the one crop of winter wheat. Their work is made easier by the brigade's twenty hand tractors or walking tractors, and four-teen threshing machines. Twenty-three pumps keep the water flowing into irrigation channels. But this is only the beginning of a mechanization program which will continue through the years.

One of the production teams is in charge of breeding silk-worms. This team tends the orchards of mulberry trees whose leaves the worms love to eat. Every day the team members gather bushels of the tenderest leaves for the worms. From the moment they hatch, the silkworms have to be taken care of to be sure they do not get too cold or too hot. As they grow larger and larger, they need more and more food until at last they stop eating and begin to spin their cocoons. When the cocoons are finished, they are ready for the processing plant in Wusih.

Other brigades care for the apple and peach orchards, the brigade piggery, and the chicken and duck farms. There are two small handicraft shops at brigade headquarters, each run by its own team. In one shop, soles are made for cloth shoes. In the other, another team of women does machine-stitched embroideries. Both products will be bought by the government.

Lai-wen works with one of the three production teams that take care of the fisheries. The fisheries are a series of ponds reclaimed from Lake Taihu. Five different species of fish, but mainly carp,

In these fisheries on the banks of Lake Taihu, harvesting is done once every six months. Five different species of fish are bred here.

are raised in the ponds. Each species lives at its own level and prefers its own kind of food so that they do not eat one another.

The Wusih fisheries teams are also in charge of the production of cultured pearls. The pearls are produced by inserting bits of sand under the shells of large oysters, which are then bred in a big underground tank. When the oysters are ready for harvesting, young women carefully pry out the pearls with long forceps. Some of the shells may contain several pearls of varying sizes and shapes.

The peasants at Ho La Brigade grow oysters which produce cultured pearls. Here a worker is carefully extracting pearls.

For recreation for their members, the brigade has organized volley ball, table tennis and basketball teams. Lai-wen, who was good at basketball in school, serves as coach as well as player.

Once a week a movie is shown at the brigade headquarters. Sometimes a Communist education team on tour for the government comes to Wusih to put on plays or other performances which have a patriotic or Communist theme. And since the town is so close, it is always possible to go in to see a movie or a live show.

Tsung-meng, who is in the sixth grade, takes an active part in the organization he joined when he was eight years old. It is the nationwide Little Red Soldier organization for children in elementary school. It is considered a great honor to belong to the Little Red Soldiers, since not every child is accepted. Those who want to join must first apply to the Little Red Soldier organization in their school. Little Red Soldier members then judge the applicants' merits and attitudes. Do they show a desire to help others? Are they sincerely interested in studying about Communism? Do they display a great loyalty to their country by being willing to work for it?

If the answers to these questions is "yes" the children are invited to join. The badge of the Little Red Soldiers is the red kerchief which they wear around their necks.

Tsung-meng never misses the political discussions which the Little Red Soldiers hold several times a week in one of the school classrooms. He helps put out the school paper, which is actually only a large blackboard on the playground. Every day, Tsung-meng and several other members arrive early to write the morning news on the blackboard.

The news consists of information about the government. One of the children also writes an editorial on Communist ideals. Others report on students who have served the people. Has a

Little Red Soldiers, led by their teacher, go out at harvest time to pick up the heads of rice left behind by the reapers.

child returned a lost purse or run errands for an elderly person, or gone out of the way to do a service for someone? That child, whether a member of the Little Red Soldiers or not, is sure to be named and praised on the blackboard.

In the adult world, local news is passed along in the same way.

Information and criticism are printed in large characters on poster-size paper which is pasted on the walls of buildings for all to read. These are known as Big Character Posters.

The Little Red Soldiers also organize skits, a glee club, an orchestra. They put on programs for Wusih and the surrounding villages. One day, they were invited to the sanitarium to perform for Tsung-meng's father and his fellow patients.

Not everything is work for the Little Red Soldiers. Sometimes they go on picnic outings. Sometimes they hike along the wooded shore of Lake Taihu, visiting scenic pavilions along the way. Sometimes they go down to the Ho La Brigade port to board a ferry that will take them to an island in the lake.

While the ferry with its red flag flying plows through the quiet waters, the children look about them. There is other traffic on the lake. Ferries like theirs are carrying more visitors to the island, a favorite recreation spot. Fishing boats are out trolling. There is an occasional small freighter or a barge filled with farm produce. On a houseboat slowly gliding by the sails are spread to the breeze, the family laundry, stretched out on bamboo poles, is flapping gaily. Lake Taihu, which is the center of a number of other lakes joined by canals, is an important transportation link with other cities.

Most of the children in Tsung-meng's class do not know yet what they want to do when they graduate. If they are asked, they answer only, "Serve the people where I am needed." But Tsung-meng knows what he wants to be—a figurine maker.

For centuries, Wusih has been famous for its clay figurine craftsmen. In the old days, figurines were made only once a year—at peach blossom time, which brought out tourists from all over China. For the tourist trade, the craftsmen, working at home, created traditional figures of the four "Olds"—generals, ministers, emperors, scholars. Since such figurines were made nowhere else in China, they were proof that the tourists had actually been to peach country.

When the tourist season was over, the figurine craftsmen had to scrape along as fuel gatherers, food hawkers and even beggars. But they guarded their secrets about the figurines from all but the members of their own families. Their skills were passed down from generation to generation. When the People's Republic of China was founded, the craftsmen were persuaded to teach their craft to classes of young apprentices so that the art would not be lost.

Today, figurine making is a full time occupation in Wusih. The figurines are sold both in China and abroad. They no longer depict the four Olds, but are gaily painted figures of fighting peasants and revolutionary heroes and heroines, chubby children and pandas.

In the old days, they were made of clay dug up from the rice paddies of the Wusih countryside. But today more and more gypsum, manufactured in Shanghai factories, is being used. It is easier to work with and lasts longer.

The figurine factory is housed in a two-story building, and Tsung-meng visits it whenever he has a chance. In the clean sunlit rooms, he stops to watch expert workers touching the plain statuettes with delicate brush strokes that will bring them to life. Old workers, past the retirement age, linger on to instruct the young apprentices.

Tsung-meng dreams of the day when he can join these apprentices. His fingers itch for the feel of the paint brush. He has an artistic bent, and his teacher advised him to apply for an apprenticeship. With her recommendation, he will be accepted if there is a vacancy for him. He can do his apprenticeship while still attending high school. By the time he graduates, he will be a full-fledged craftsman.

Apprentices at the Wusih figurine factory, under the supervision of old artisans, learn how to create the colorful figurines for which Wusih has long been famous.

If there is no opening in the figurine factory right away, he will continue his high school education. Hopefully, by the time he graduates, he may be able to enter the factory. If not, he can be sure there will be work of some kind waiting for him, though it may not be what he wants. There is no unemployment in China today.

TSINAN, CITY OF SPRINGS

Pao-lang lives in the ancient city of Tsinan which stands on the lower reaches of the Yellow River. How different the surrounding countryside is from the lush green fields and shimmering lakes, canals and streams of the Land of Rice and Fish farther south. Broad yellow plains stretch out on all sides, except where the rocky Tai Shan hills rise to the southeast of the city. Part of the province of Shantung, in which Tsinan is located, was once a rocky offshore island. Since then, it has been connected to the mainland by a low-lying plain built up of Yellow River silt.

Over the centuries, the Yellow River and its tributaries created the entire North China Plain. During the heavy rains, the Yellow River and other streams carried the fine rich soil from the north-west regions of China down through the mountains to the shallow waters of the ocean. Layer after layer of river silt built up the bed of the ocean until it formed a broad plain which today covers some 200,000 square miles. This is the North China Plain.

Long ago when the first peasants started farming on the plain, they built dikes to keep the Yellow River from overflowing. When the river could not spread its load of silt as it had in the past, the silt dropped instead to the river bottom. As the centuries went by, the river bed was raised higher and higher by the silt layers. This meant the peasants had to make the dikes higher still. Now there are places where the dikes rise some twenty-five feet above the surface of the plain. Peasants looking up can sometimes see the sails of boats passing overhead.

The river is wide but not deep enough for large ships. Motor boats can travel it. But Tsinan does not need the river to be an

Soon after the People's Republic of China was founded, in 1949, the citizens of Tsinan began a "greening" program—planting shade trees along the main streets. Today, many of the buildings are completely hidden by the trees.

important transportation center. Railways connect it to many cities, from north to south and east to west.

Parts of the city show the influence of the Germans and Japanese who lived there in earlier days. European-style buildings

line some of the streets, which are shaded with trees planted during the first years of the greening program.

Down the streets clomp large horses and small Mongolian ponies and donkeys hauling carts of produce or loads of lumber for the building construction that is continually going on. Horses and donkeys, which are the chief form of transport in the north, are seldom seen in the south where the climate does not agree with them.

Pao-lang's home is in the old Chinese part of the city, the most scenic section. Tsinan has long been known as the City of Springs because there are so many here. Parks are built around almost every one of them. One of Pao-lang's favorites is the Leaping Spring Park. Once Leaping Spring Park was a Buddhist center. The temple which stands in it was built in the tenth century A.D. Now restored, it still mirrors its red colonnades in the pool waters as it did long ago.

In the old days, the temple grounds were the scene of monthly fairs where craftsmen and peasants gathered to sell their wares. Those fairs are a thing of the past. But the park is still crowded with people all week long. This is because not all the workers get days off at the same time.

The place is especially beautiful in the autumn when the chrysanthemums are blooming. The cultivation of the chrysanthemum has always been a fine art with the Chinese. More than three thousand varieties have been developed to date. Behind the glass walls of hothouses, where the most delicate flowers bloom, Pao-lang sees two young art students sketching the flowers. One day, their designs may appear on an embroidered tapestry, a piece of lacquerware, or fine porcelain.

There is another side to Tsinan, however. Since the building of a thermal power station nearby, it is also becoming industrialized.

The scenic parks of China are always crowded with people.

Already there are iron and steel mills. Other factories manufacture agricultural equipment, machine tools and motor vehicles.

Pao-lang's father works in the pencil factory which he helped start back in 1951. At that time, the country was so poor that the government could not provide enough jobs for everyone. So forty unemployed men, including Pao Lang's father, got together to discuss what they could make that would sell in a country like China. When they realized the emphasis the government was placing on teaching people how to read and write, they felt they had found an answer. Writing requires pencils, so why not manufacture pencils? The men turned their homes into workshops and began making pencils, doing most of the labor by hand.

Today the pencil factory has grown into a large building equipped with machinery so that it manufactures about two hundred million pencils a year. And it employs some six hundred workers, half of them women.

When Pao-lang's mother was younger, she also worked in the factory. But since then, she has received training as a pharmacist and now is employed in a hospital making up pills and filling prescriptions. The medicines she makes are sold at less than cost, and the most expensive is never more than a few pennies.

Pao-lang goes to the Tsinan No. 22 Middle School (high school), which was established in 1958, and now has almost three thousand students. School begins at seven-thirty in the morning with a brisk round of calisthenics. Classes last until eleven-thirty, and then begin again at two and continue until four. But most of the students stay on until five-thirty for the after-school activities.

Pao-lang studies politics, Chinese language, mathematics, English, physics and chemistry. Five laboratories enable the students to put the theories they learn in physics and chemistry classes to practical use. As China strives to modernize, greater emphasis than ever before is being placed on technological and scientific

City high school students spend part of every vacation in the countryside doing manual labor side by side with peasants.

education. And Pao-lang's teachers are impressed with the aptitude she shows for physics.

A small factory attached to the school allows the students to do the manual work required of them. Every year during their two-month vacation, the students also spend some time working in a factory or on a commune. Pao-lang spent part of her last vacation on the banks of the Yellow River. One of her chores was to check

As China tries to modernize her industries, greater emphasis than ever before is being placed on technological and scientific education.

for cracks or breaks in the dikes so they could be repaired.

Keeping a constant lookout for weak points in the dikes is important because when the river is in flood a single crack can quickly become a gaping hole through which the angry torrent pours. In the past this happened often, drowning thousands of people and causing millions more to die from the famine which followed. But shortly after the People's Republic was established, peasants, workers and soldiers got together to strengthen the dikes. Today, the weaker stretches are reenforced with concrete embankments.

Several times a week, soldiers of the People's Liberation Army stationed near the village where Pao-lang is spending her summer come to train the peasants in the use of firearms. Almost all the people of China are receiving basic military training. They make up a force known as the People's Militia. In case of invasion or all-out war, they will be able to fight beside the People's Liberation Army.

Pao-lang's older sister Tai-mei joined the army after her graduation from high school. Young women as well as young men are accepted. Physical and moral requirements are strict. Not everyone who applies is admitted. As always, the yardstick is whether or not the applicant is willing to serve the people.

Once the military profession was considered the lowest in China, and soldiers were hated because they murdered, looted and raped the peasants whose villages they occupied. But from the very beginning of the Revolution, Mao Tsetung laid down rules of behavior for the newly formed People's Liberation Army, which became the code for all Communist Chinese soldiers. The code included such rules as helping peasants rather than preying on them, never stealing, and always paying for food and other things instead of taking them.

The People's Liberation Army has lived up to these rules. Soldiers work with the peasants at sowing and harvest times. They help with canal and bridge building. They plant and tend their own fields, so they can supply their own food and do not have to ask for supplies from the peasants in whose commune they live.

The army runs hospitals which care for civilians as well as soldiers. Army stations in remote regions send out medical units to care for isolated families. Cultural units tour the countryside performing revolutionary ballads and folk dances in remote villages which otherwise would have no entertainment.

Tai-mei is a member of such a group. She is stationed in the far northwest and seldom comes home. But when she arrives for a visit, her whole neighborhood turns out to greet and honor her.

When Tai-mei comes home, she likes to visit Pao-lang's school to coach her younger sister and her friends. They have formed a little amateur dance troupe, and spend hours practicing after school. They learn their dance numbers by watching professional performers. They copy the routines, and criticize one another's performance until they are almost as polished as the professionals themselves. Sometimes their teacher coaches them, and on occasion members from the professional troupe visit the school to give pointers.

Pao-lang and her friends are often asked to give performances in factories and out-of-the-way villages, which do not have city entertainment. The day their troupe arrives in Fei-niao's village, there is great excitement. The village has few opportunities for entertainment because it stands in an isolated valley among rock-strewn hills, not far from Tsinan.

The village houses are made of yellow adobe bricks and are as dusty looking as the valley in which they stand. Narrow dirt lanes separate the houses. In the summer, they bake under the hot

The houses in this village in north China are made of yellow adobe bricks, and are separated from one another by narrow dirt lanes.

cloudless sunlight, but the winters are often freezing. When Arctic winds blow down from the high Mongolian plains, the air is filled with a fine haze of gritty dust that stings Fei-niao's eyes and throat.

Then all the villagers put on layer after layer of padded clothing. And to protect their heads and ears, many of the children wear woolen caps with ear flaps. It is nice at such times to have a warm bed on which to sleep.

Fei-niao's bed, which she shares with other members of the family, is a long brick platform with an oven underneath. She and her brothers gather brush and leaves for fuel. Early in the evening, their father builds a fire in the oven, and by the time the family is ready to go to bed, the brick platform is warm. Wrapped up in their coverlets, the family will spend a comfortable night.

Fei-niao's village is not a rich one. But it can raise enough wheat and millet, sorghum and sweet potatoes to make a comfortable living for itself. It was not always so. Along with other poor villages throughout the valley, its people had always lived at the edge of starvation.

The problem was climate. The rocky hills which enclose the valley block off most of the rain clouds, forcing them to drop their moisture on the other side. There the land is lush and green and laced with streams, while Fei-niao's valley suffers drought.

After the founding of the People's Republic, the peasants of the valley joined forces in a single commune. With spades and picks, dynamite, and baskets to carry off the earth, they dug and blasted and scooped their way through the hills to form several tunnels. Now water is brought through the tunnels from the far side to irrigate their crops. Irrigation insures good crops.

Next, work teams began digging out the rocks which covered the hills. They used them to build terrace walls. Then they filled the terraces with good earth and planted sweet potatoes. Today, in the growing season, hills and valley form a patchwork of rich shimmering shades of green.

But now it is mid-fall and the colors are somber. The grain has

This small girl not only minds her baby brother, but she also helps by carting freshly dug sweet potatoes to central depots. ▶

been harvested. Almost all the sweet potatoes have been dug from the ground. Small children munch on boiled potatoes instead of candy. Older people and children gather up the harvest of potatoes in wicker baskets and heap them at the corners of the fields. They will be washed and cut into thin slices and spread on trays to dry.

To help celebrate their harvest season, the peasants of Fei-niao's village have invited Pao-lang's amateur troupe to perform for them. Peasants from other villages around the valley join the crowd that has gathered in the cleanly swept communal courtyard.

The audience is all there by the time Pao-lang and her troupe arrive, some on foot, others on bicycles. They carry their costumes in wicker baskets. And Fei-niao's mother offers them her home as a place to change.

And so the performance begins. Each dance uses a different costume—blue slacks with red scarves to do the red scarf dance, blue slacks with aprons and baskets to do the harvest dance. Last of all, in ankle-length pale green dresses, the costume of the Korean minority peoples that live in northeast China, the girls do a Korean folk dance. This is only one of many minority folk songs and dances which have been popularized in China. It is part of the government's campaign to foster harmony and respect between the minority peoples and the majority Han. Today China calls all her citizens Chinese, just as America calls hers Americans. But in the past the Han looked on themselves as the only true Chinese. From their homes along the Yellow and Yangtze Rivers they pushed China's borders outward, conquering groups of non-Han peoples along the way. These are the minority peoples in modern China.

Every time Pao-lang's troupe comes to Fei-niao's village to perform, they coach the peasant girls. One day these young women

Chinese students like these are learning the folk dances of many minority peoples in a campaign to further understanding between the various races in China. This is a Korean folk dance from the northeast region.

will be able to form their own troupe, and the people of the valley will have more entertainment.

During their stay in the village, Pao-lang and her classmates help the villagers with sweeping and carrying water, slicing sweet potatoes and doing other country chores. There's also time for a little sightseeing. Beyond the village, in the most desolate part of the valley, stands an ancient Buddhist monastery which is being preserved by the government as an historical monument.

The main part of the monastery itself is in ruins. But the Four Door Pagoda for which the place is famous still stands on its knoll overlooking the valley. And the four hundred or so carvings of

The carved Buddhas in the Cliff of Ten Thousand Buddhas outside Tsinan represent donations from people who were rewarded in this way by the artist monks who lived here.

These stupas or prayer pagodas mark the cemetery of Buddhist monks who lived in the monastery connected with the Cliff of Ten Thousand Buddhas and the Four Door Pagoda.

the Buddha are on a cliff near the monastery. It is called the Cliff of Ten Thousand Buddhas. The carvings are very old, but they still look down in rows from the cliff face. Each Buddha represents the donation of some wealthy person whom the monk sculptors honored with a carving—the more important the person and the bigger the donation, the larger the carving.

The valley itself is filled with stupas, or prayer pagodas (grave-shrines) that mark the graves of the monks who lived and died here over the centuries. Religion is not encouraged in China today, but worship is permitted. There are only a few Buddhists in China, and even fewer Moslems and Christians.

Pao-lang's grandmother is still a Buddhist. She believes that she has been born again and again in the past and will be born again and again in the future. She is convinced that the quality of each new life she lives will depend on the merit she achieved in the preceding one.

Pao-lang does not understand her grandmother's beliefs, the beliefs that led thousands of monks to live and die in this desolate spot. The wind blows fitfully through the rows of tall cedars planted in recent years during the greening program. It rustles through the leaves of the six-hundred-year-old banyan tree that overshadows the Four Door Pagoda and was planted here at the time the pagoda was built.

On some of the newly built terraces that surround the valley, rows of young apple trees, bare now of leaves, stand like scarecrows. But in the spring, they will burst into pale pink blossoms and in the early fall will bear fruit—apples. How those old monks would have relished that fresh fruit. Neither they nor any of the people of the valley had seen apples here in the old days.

面对这些阻力和责难，这些年来，在党的关怀和鼓励下，我一方面坚持天象观测，进行业余天文科学研究，

天文观测是专门研究机意把自己掌握的一点科学知识贡献给农村的社会主义事业。平时，利用政治夜校向群

构是不够的，需要千千天文科学常识，**讲解一些天象**，这有助于破除少数群众中的迷信思想，防止阶级敌人

可能一帆风〜败的文现象造谣破坏。我还给群众讲解二十四个节气的原理和简单的推算方法，开展一些

存在"蛇夫！星群"农业生产服务的活动。比如广泛收集民间气象谚语，利用"蚂蟥瓶"等土设备，办了"

回否定了。以后还有两"，结合观察风云物象，及时预报灾害性天气，使生产队几年都没有发生早稻烂秧现象

8.
PEKING THE MAGNIFICENT

Pao-lang and her troupe have just been chosen to go to Peking to take part in the nationwide cultural meet which is being held in the capital. There will be amateur and professional troupes from all over China performing folk dances, Chinese operas, ballets and acrobatics. Each commune and city district has voted for its best performers to represent it. Pao-lang and her friends feel honored that they are among those chosen.

Though passenger planes connect Tsinan with Peking as well as with other important cities around China, the young women will travel by train. Their families and schoolmates come to the station to see them off.

The train pulls out and rolls north through a flat golden plain. Looking out the windows, the young women see clusters of yellow adobe houses standing in the midst of harvested fields. Now that the slack period is here, people are free to do reclamation projects. Work teams with spades and wheelbarrows are digging an irrigation ditch along the edge of the highway that parallels the road.

Only an occasional truck travels the highway. The chief means of transportation in northern China is still the horse. Horses pulling carts laden with produce move in a steady procession down the road, headed for cities along the way. Occasionally the train

whips by long rows of haystacks whose peaked tops rise like miniature huts above a village wall.

Here and there, the train stops at a station to take on and discharge passengers and goods—ducks and geese in pens, bales of cotton, bags of rice. On the porch of one small station, the station mistress squats over a bucket washing clothes. She is just a pigtailed teenager only a little older than Pao-lang and her companions. Her bicycle, which is her means of transportation to and from work, leans against a pillar of the porch.

(opposite, top) In the slack period of the year, teams of peasants work on reclamation projects such as this irrigation ditch on the North China Plain.

(opposite, bottom) Clusters of adobe houses dot the flat North China Plain.

(right) Farm-bred ducks in a crate wait to be loaded aboard the train for city markets or restaurants.

In the railroad yards beyond stand open cars piled with lumber which will soon be on its way to construction sites in the cities. The wood comes from tree farms in Chekiang Province to the south. The trees were planted some twenty-five years before and are now ready for harvesting. Each tree that is cut down is replaced by a sapling.

Whenever the train stops for longer periods of time, the girls get off to do some calisthenics. Up and down the platform other travelers are also working out the kinks from legs and backs.

Belching smoke stacks on the outskirts of Peking reveal the growing number of industrial plants around the city, and contrast strongly with the carter of hay in the foreground.

A station mistress, just a pigtailed teenager, washes clothes on the floor of a small train station which she supervises.

Peking itself stands in the midst of the golden plain, and as the train nears the outskirts of the city, belching smoke stacks appear against the skyline. Industrialization has come to the capital suburbs, but the city itself is protected from pollution. It is the heart and the head of modern China, the hub of this vast country. Those who live in Peking feel themselves honored. Outsiders dream of the day they can pay a visit here.

Pao-lang and her troupe are now among the fortunate ones. They are taken to a hostel where other troupes are gathered. All of them will perform before a huge crowd. Afterwards, members of the crowd will be free to voice their criticisms of the performance. The troupes will also criticize and coach one another. Pao-lang and her friends will learn many new steps and techniques.

But they are interested in more than dancing. Now that they are in storied Peking, they want to see all they can of the great city. One of the Peking home troupes shows them around. The first place they visit is the Royal Palace Museum which was once the home of the emperors. It was known as the Great Within, or the Forbidden City, so called because no commoner on pain of death was allowed within its walls uninvited.

In front of the red walls that enclose the Forbidden City stretches a vast square called Tien An Men Square. The massive gate that separates the Forbidden Palace from the Square is known as Tien An Men Gate. It was in 1949, on the rostrum atop the gate, that Mao Tsetung read the proclamation of the founding of the People's Republic of China. Now his body lies in the southern part of the square in a mausoleum built of marble.

On the west rises the Great Hall of the People. In its gigantic banquet rooms, Chinese government officials welcome dignitaries from foreign countries. In the huge auditorium, delegates from all over the country gather periodically to discuss their government's business and to cast their votes.

Groups of people are walking back and forth across Tien An Men square. Some are on their way to work. Others are headed for Chairman Mao's mausoleum to pay their respects before going on through Tien An Men gate. A woman on her way to market wheels a homemade wooden cart in which a child stands, bundled up against the cold, for the fall brings nippy weather to Peking. The cart is large enough to hold packages as well as the child.

Inside Tien An Men gate, the present gives way to a royal past.

Sightseers strolling through the Forbidden City, now the Palace Museum, look at the great palaces where emperors once held court.

There are broad terraces and marble bridges with carved railings. Red lacquered, golden roofed wooden palaces stand on the terraces. All has been carefully restored so that it looks just as it did when the emperors lived here.

Years of work went into the building of the royal city, which was first made the capital of the great Mongolian Empire under Kublai Khan in 1264. The Great Within was rebuilt by the Ming Dynasty

113

A woman wheels her child in a homemade wooden cart. There are many such go-carts in China.

which came to power in 1368. The Ming emperors were determined to make it even grander than it was as the Mongol city of Kublai Khan. Hundreds of people and mules pulled mile-long ropes to haul the stone and marble from quarries in the northern mountains. Others hauled huge timbers cut from rare trees in the far southern provinces of Yunnan and Kweichow.

Two hundred thousand skilled workmen built terraces and set up railings. Other workmen raised the wooden palaces which were lacquered red. Roofers topped the buildings with the golden yellow tiles, decorating roof ridges and eaves with tiles of other colors.

Woodworkers carved the bas-reliefs on the pillars. Sculptors carved similar bas-reliefs on the marble balustrades. The chief figure they carved was the five-clawed dragon, emblem of the emperor. Its sinuous coils wound among waves and clouds and pomegranates—all good-luck symbols.

Workers in bronze cast four- to five-foot-high replicas of the royal dragon, the longevity crane, the powerful lion, the fierce mystical khiling and the honest tortoise. These were set upon the terraces among huge bronze incense burners.

The largest of the throne rooms, the Hall of Assured Harmony, was the audience chamber of the emperor. Here envoys came from distant vassal states bringing rich tributes—elephants, artifacts of pure gold, great slabs of jade, rich furs, fine pearls. They presented the gifts to the monarch, making him the "ninefold kowtow," a bowing that left them lying prostrate on the floor. And every envoy went away with a gift richer than the one he had brought so that he would sing the praises of the mightiest ruler on earth.

Scattered among the royal buildings are exquisitely landscaped parks with ancient trees and neatly trimmed shrubbery. In the past, right where Pao-lang and her friends are sightseeing, court ladies once strolled in beautiful embroidered gowns. Saffron-robed eunuchs scurried on errands, and royal children played— the girls in long embroidered dresses, the boys in ankle-length pantaloons, vests and gowns.

It looked like a happy scene, but actually the world of the Great Within was full of intrigue and tragedy. No one in the royal city

was safe, not even the emperor himself. Those in the worst danger were his children who were only pawns in a deadly game. Murder by poison, dagger, or strangulation was a common occurrence as power hungry concubines united with eunuchs to reach a place of power.

As the Son of Heaven, the Emperor was the religious as well as political head of the empire. The Temple of Heaven where he went every year to pray for good harvests was built by thousands of skilled workmen.

The emperor's pleasures were lavish, as Pao-lang and her friends discover when they pay a visit to the royal summer palaces which stand outside Peking on an artificial lake called West Lake.

Here the last empress, the widow Tze Hsi, built a marble pleasure boat with monies which were supposed to be used by the royal navy. The dowager empress entertained her court in the marble boat and in her cluster of summer palaces with their outdoor theater. Often she visited the Buddhist temple that rises on the hill above the lake, or took her court sailing on it, accompanied by musicians who entertained the royal group. Pao-lang and her friends stroll through the galleries of the marble ship. Then, for a few pennies they rent a boat and go rowing on the lake which was once reserved for royalty. On their way back to the city, they stop to visit the tombs of the Ming emperors. The cemetery which houses the tombs has been turned into a public park. It is reached by a road lined by huge stone figures of lions, camels and other creatures that were put there to guard the bodies of the dead, which have long since been removed.

Families enjoy rowing on scenic West Lake outside Peking, once reserved for royal boating parties.

Wandering through the park where there are museums holding relics of the past, descending the long flights of stone steps into the cool darkness of the tombs, Pao-lang is glad that she lives today. As her parents and teachers have often pointed out to her, it was only the rich who enjoyed the good things of life, while millions of people starved to provide them with those good things. And she is grateful that in this new China no one starves while others live in luxury.

118

Of course, no trip to Peking is complete without seeing the Great Wall which lies about twenty-five miles north of the city. About twenty-one feet wide and eighteen feet high, it marches across north China in a winding course more than eighteen hundred miles long. At regular distances, the wall is broken by watch towers from which sentries could look out at the Mongolian plains to the north. At any sign of a nomad gathering, the soldiers guarding the passes and the wall would be alerted.

Hundreds of thousands of people built the wall, braving snow and sleet and hot summer suns. Thousands upon thousands died before the project was completed. Today it is regarded as one of

The Great Wall, which lies about 25 miles north of Peking, winds across north China's Inner Mongolia region, a distance of some 1,800 miles.

the foremost man-made wonders of the world. And all Chinese are proud of the humble laborers who built it at so great a cost of human life and suffering.

There are always visitors on the wall. Parents bring their children, some of them tiny babies. Soldiers come to jog up and down the steep inclines to keep fit. An old woman whose feet were partially bound has hobbled here to look out wistfully across the misty mountains. And because human beings are alike the world over, Pao-lang and her friends see the names of modern visitors, probably students like themselves, carved into the ancient stone.

On the way back from the wall, the young women stop at the Peking zoo to see the giant pandas which pause now and then to look back at the spectators with sad clown eyes. They are found in the wild only in China and are extremely rare. But in recent years, the zoo keepers have been able to get captive pandas to mate and produce living offspring. Perhaps this will be the means of saving the giant panda from extinction should it ever vanish from the wild.

Before the girls leave Peking, they visit the National Minorities Institute to learn more folk dances from the students there. Several institutes of this kind have been set up in China to educate the minority peoples, most of whom live around the borders. There are Koreans in the northeast, Uighurs and Kazakhs in far western Sinkiang, Tibetans in Tibet. Many different nationalities, such as the Miao, the Yi, and the Thai, live in southwest China.

The students at the institute have been selected by their communities for their outstanding public spirit. At the school, they continue to wear their native dress and speak their native language. Food is especially prepared to suit their tastes. Everything is done to make them feel at home during their six months' stay here.

A giant panda at the Peking zoo surveys the staring spectators with sad clown eyes. China is very concerned about preserving this rare animal, which has long been threatened with extinction.

Workmen excavating for an underground classroom at the Minorities Institute, Peking.

They are given lessons in reading and writing, both in their own language and in that of the Han. They also take advanced courses in agriculture, technology and medicine. When they return to their own homes, they will be able to play an important part in the development of their communities.

One of the things the Minorities Institute students point out to Pao-lang and her friends is the underground classroom which is being dug. The classroom is one of a number of other underground rooms connected by a vast complex of tunnels. The tunnels, rooms and first-aid stations which underlie Peking were dug and equipped by volunteer workers in their spare time.

Pao-lang, her family and friends helped dig similar tunnels and rooms beneath their own city of Tsinan. Almost every city in China has a similar network of tunnels. The Chinese have made these shelters for protection in case of bombardment. If their country should be invaded, the people would go underground to fight a guerrilla action. Pao-lang and her classmates have been taught that the chief threat to world peace is the Soviet Union. They are daily warned to be vigilant.

The Soviet Union and China were friendly up to 1956. After that date, the Chinese claimed that the Soviet Union grew careless in the practice of Communist ideals and was becoming too friendly with nations whom the Chinese considered to be worst enemies of Communism. The two nations argued over this until their dispute became so bitter that it erupted in fighting along the borders they shared. By 1963 the rift had grown too wide to bridge.

Before Pao-lang leaves Peking, she visits the city's two famous universities. One is the University of Peking. The other is Tsinghua University, well known throughout China for its technological courses.

When Pao-lang graduates from high school, she would like to attend Tsinghua University. If her grades in the sciences are high enough, if the professors feel she is qualified and if there is room for her there, she will be able to go. Of course there are other fine universities in large Chinese cities such as Shanghai, Hankow and Kuangchow. But it is to Peking that Pao-lang would like to

return. The atmosphere of the beautiful city has entered her blood.

Meanwhile, she and her friends ride home again through the golden countryside. They will have many stories to tell of their stay in the capital. But life will never be quite the same for them again. They have seen magnificent Peking.

PRONUNCIATION GUIDE

Chiang Kai-shek — Jee-ahng Ki-shek
Chin-mai — Jin-mi
Chu-lai — Choo-li
Fei-niao — Fay-nee-ao
Hai-feng — Hi-fuhng
Han — Hahn
Hankow — Hahn-koh
Hsi-fan — Shee-fahn
Hsin Hui — Sheen Huay
Hung Hsiu-chuan — Hoong Sheeu-juahn
Kazakh — Kah-zahk
Kiangmen — Jee-ahng-muhn
Kit-ho — Geet-hoh
Kuangchow — Gwahng-joh
Kublai Khan — Koob-li Kahn
Kwangtung — Gwahng-toong
Kweichow — Gway-joh
Lai-feng — Li-fuhng
Lai-wen — Li-wuhn
Mao Tsetung — Mao Dzuh-doong
Mei-li — May-lee
Miao — Mee-ao
Ming-li — Ming-lee
Pao-lang — Bao-lahng
Pei — Bay
Peking — Bay-jing

Shanghai — Shahng-hi
Si — See
Sinkiang — Sin-jiang
Sung (Dynasty) — Soong
Sun Yat-sen — Soon Yaht-sen
Tachai — Da-ji
Taching — Da-jing
Tai-mei — Ti-may
Tai-ming — Ti-ming
Taiping (rebellion) — Ti-ping
Ta-lai — Tah-li
Tan — Tahn
Tek Ya Na — Tehk Yah Nah
Thai — Ti
Tsinan — Jee-nahn
Tsinghua — Jing-huah
Tsunh-meng — Tsoong-meng
Tung — Doong
Tze Hsi — Dzuh Shee
Uighur — Wee-gur
Whangpoo — Whahng-poo
Yangtze — Yahng-dzuh
Yi — Yee
Yuan Shih-kai — Yuahn Shr-ki
Yunnan — Yuhn-nahn

INDEX